the rain sings for you

DEEPIKA SINGH

INDIA • SINGAPORE • MALAYSIA

ISBN 979-8-89588-286-3

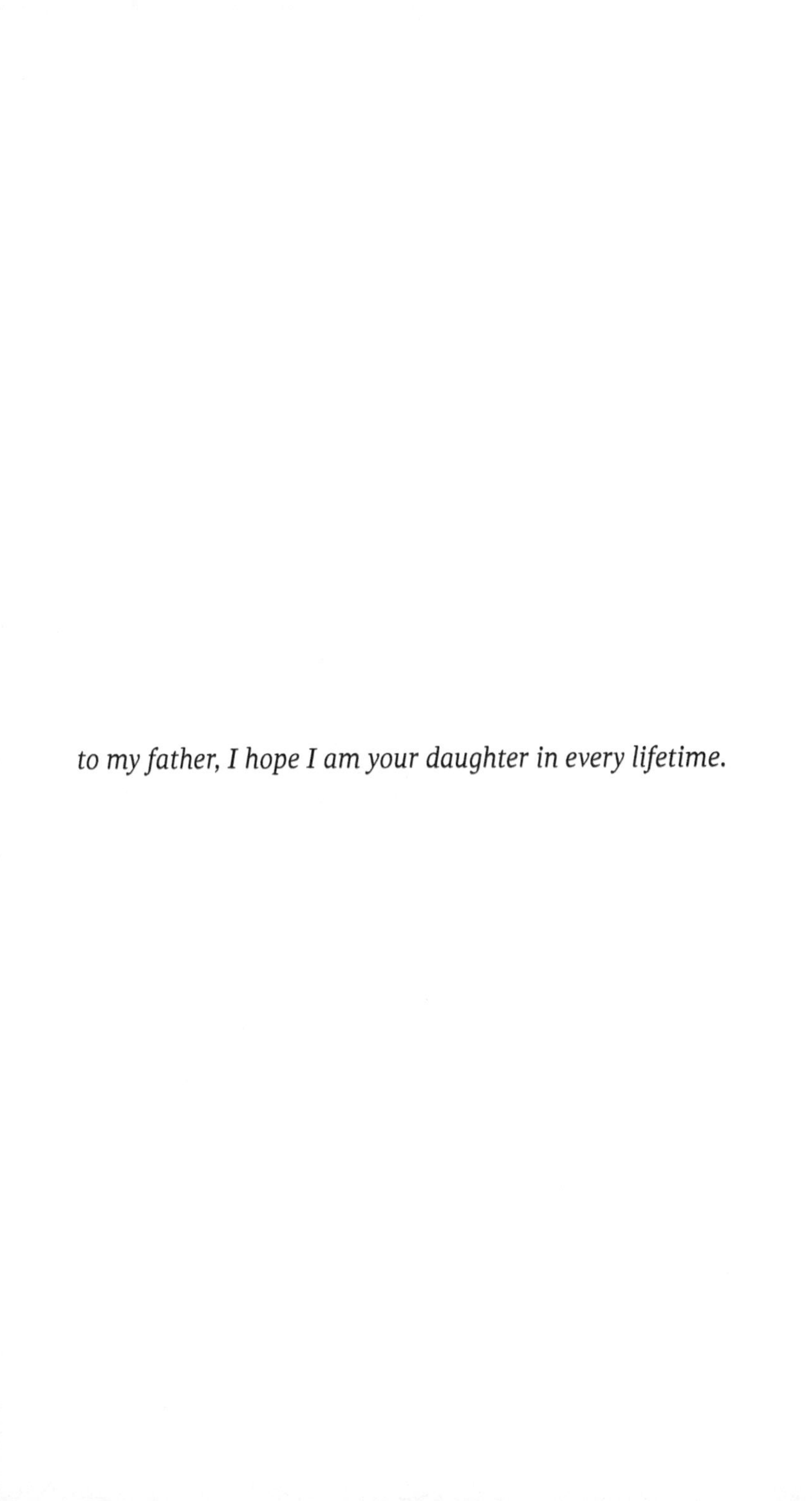

to my father, I hope I am your daughter in every lifetime.

A Note to the Readers

Dear reader,

Publishing my work always felt like a faraway dream, like the finish line of a marathon I never thought I would even run.

But here I am and here you are.

Even as you are currently holding my book in your hands and reading this, I'm probably (most definitely) sitting somewhere still in shock that this actually happened; nevertheless, I am so immensely grateful.

I've poured my heart and soul into this book and before you go further, I have one tiny request; don't just read the words. *Feel them.*

all my love,
Deepika

to be alive is to be chaos.

— Lucas jones.

1.

and if this is the last time these hands
ever hold a pen
let my words be for you
let me write; not about the color of your eyes
or about how you pin up your hair
or the way you make me smile
let me write instead
about the sheer beauty of your existence
let me write about how
wishes do indeed come true
because sometimes it feels like
I wished you into life
let me write about fate
no, not just any fate
but the fate of you and I
linked together
till the last atom of the world
crumbles.

2.

defined by the past
we live for the future
present blurs, present fades.

3.

I came out of my mother's womb
not crying or screaming
but begging to be loved
but see, I was born on a battlefield
in between soldiers waging war
more familiar to the curve of a blade
than my own mother's soft hands
then yes my father, he wields the sword
I tell him not to bother
his words can cut more sharp
and so the armies fight
metal clinks, blood spills
the little girl in the middle
is not much more than an afterthought
some battles, she wins
some battles, he wins
but the war—the war, I lose.

4.

I love you in yellow, you said
you loved me in all colors, I knew
now I have left our kaleidoscopic land to be in a gutter of
black and white.

5.

till every bit of you is
every bit of me,
till all I see is you and
all you see is me.

6.

alas, this melancholy
makes a garden inside me
and the monster that I am, I water that garden religiously.

7.

wake up, beautiful
it's summer again
icecreams and bicycles
and sundresses and sweat
with the sun on my back
and flipflops on your feet
we'll write our names in the sand
and make castles together
then live in them forever
and when the real world comes knocking
we'll pretend we're under the covers.

8.

what a wretched liar I am
when I say,
I have nothing left to lose
whilst you still breathe.

9.

I bled like the ink of the pen with which I wrote; swift
and smooth
I wept like a newborn in the cradle of it's mother's
arms; ungrateful and unknowing
and I left my blood and tears for all to see,
not to admire but to experiment
so, examine the salt of my tears,
scrutinize the iron of my blood
and tell the world
how the girl with icy fingers and molten eyes,
was never quite right
something off in the way she lived;
always for the future, never in the present.
something off in the way she spoke;
scared even of her own shadow
scared that her wings would fail her
so, she never flew at all
she never flew at all
and when the time came to remove
her essence off the world
It did not take more
than a fistful of water
you cannot remove what never was.

10.

indeed, i want love
for who does not?
but I do not wish for it to be fleeting
I want my love to be all consuming
devastating in it's eternity
I want my love to burn with the ferocity of a
thousand suns
I want my love to sink it's claws in my skin,
release it's poison in my blood
I want my love to be a parasite and I, it's host
I want my love to be
the death of me
or I do not want it at all.

11.

the rain sings
sings just for me
forevermore, I am lost in its symphony.

12.

when I die don't look for me in the stars and certainly not the moon-- look for me in the weathered pages of my favorite stories and my most beloved poems, look for me in all the dreams I dreamed and all the defeat I faced, look for me in the God I didn't believe in and the prayers I never understood, look for me in all the love I gave out and the rage I kept within. but most importantly when you look for me, *don't go too far.* just sit. sit and read aloud a verse from the book I kept in my nightstand and when the too cold wind moulds to your body like a lover's embrace

know, my darling you have found me.

13.

I've lived
six thousand two hundred and nine days
but I remember only one
the day you held my hand in yours and
showed me the stars.

14.

I am a seashell at your favorite beach getting washed
away
by the waves again and again
but when I'm back at shore, back at home
I wait for you to pick me up
and put me in your collection.

15.

I have you
to love and to cherish
to hate and to resent
but not to keep
never to keep.

16.

sometimes
I want to be
that rusty coin
in your wallet
you never use
or throw away.

17.

delicate heartstrings
can't tangle them up now
indecisive and confused
you become my sixth sense.

18.

they write scriptures
of ancient gods on my skin
and make me a holy shrine
no longer just a selfish human
l am a god to be worshiped
and they worship me like the most hypocritical
of devotees, only when their guilt needs to be erased
and only when their sins need to be washed.

19.

paper, white as a dove
and just as gentle too
I write on it from top to bottom
a web of blue over seamless white
but my ink is not yet finished
so then I write on the walls
but the walls are only four
and my ink is not yet finished
then I write on myself
but my skin only stretches so far
and my ink is not yet finished
so I write on the whole damned world
I stain the universe with the weight of my words
still, my ink does not finish.

20.

in the dark
when shadows whisper
and the devils fight
no sin is sinful
all is forgotten
all is forgiven.

21.

you've pierced my soul in half
one part, yours and yours alone
the other, belonging to no one but myself
I try to stitch them together
with needle and thread
but my hands are too slippery
and there is blood, so much blood
I never heal
perhaps, some wounds are too severe
some consequence, too high.

22.

a lifetime with you
I would live
I would love
and forget it's a dream
If you never wake me up.

23.

I loved many oceans
but I drowned only
in the depth of yours
for that, if history makes a villain out of me
then a villain I shall be.

24.

in the wake
of your destruction
I am left behind
to watch infinity
turn *finite*.

25.

thunder hollers
and the wind cries out
rain wears armor
and the sea draws it's sword
all ready to wage war on my behalf
but how do l tell them?
the world is not my enemy
I am my own.

26.

I have been standing
at the edge of a cliff
ever since
while life paused around me
not brave enough
to take a step further
not brave enough
to take one back.

27.

each day, the flames burn brighter
induced by- your arrogance and my ignorance
you tell me it could be worse
but darling, you're just sunburnt
whilst my whole house is down in ashes.

28.

and even the gods must fear us now
for you and I together
we are nothing less than
immortal.

29.

often too many times
I have found myself
With a shovel in hand
and mud on my boots
burying my love for
you
in the ground.

30.

this girl I know
draws constellations on her prison bars
a futile attempt to reach the stars
but her tower's as tall as rapunzel's
and hair not as long
and prince not as patient
in her tower, she sits frozen
a prisoner of time, a victim of love
and all the townsfolk,
they want to burn her at the stake
say she's a witch, a blotch on their perfect silks
but the girl I know?
she knows just one spell
the one used to curse herself
and many have vowed to break that curse
but it has spread too far,
black tar in her veins.

31.

he fights for the golden crown
and the golden crown is very pretty, indeed
but the kingdom that comes with it
is nothing more than rubble and ash
yet the world lets him fight
better not to tell a man dying of thirst
that the last drop of water ever left is poisonous.

32.

I slit my throat for you
when you were thirsty
only to hear complaints
about the salt of my
blood.

33.

carve all your hopes
on my skin
and everywhere I go
I'll carry proof with me
that you too,
were once a dreamer.

34.

who will love the rotten girls
and the worthless boys?
their claws sharp and bloody
retracting from wounds
given by their own makers
who will shelter the discarded children?
for the rain always
falls heavier on them,
mudded boots follow them home-but no,
they do not have a home
who will be home to the cursed children?
who will remember the ones destined to be forgotten?
or will their souls forever be lost to the god that
condemned them?

35.

hear hear, death has spoken his terms
he denies you, sweet angel
till you've paid all your debts
so say all your I love yous,
grieve all your losses,
pray one last time on shooting stars
and wear the cloak of acceptance
so when death does come
to stare you in the eye
you stare right back
serve him tea and your most dazzling smile.

36.

so my dove, don't be bitter
if this life can't hold our love
I will find you in another
we'll watch sunsets together
and drink from paper straws
I'll draw hearts next to your name
evertime I see fogged glass
in that life, we will not be so tragic
and I will not be so poetic
in that life, we'll just be two people
two people bound to each other *forever*

37.

I will not promise to love you
till the end of my days
because my days will end
my love will not.

38.

my darling, you must know
how I close my eyes
everytime you walk by
because I cannot bear the sight of you
so unblemished, so untainted
while I lie here
drenched from head to toe
in the ugly color of
heartbreak.

39.

I hear my diary
weeping
in the quiet of the night
sometimes
for even it cannot contain
all the love I have lost

40.

my phantom love
even when we are
just cosmic dust
floating in the skies
I will always feel you
I will always rue you.

41.

nostalgia wraps tightly around
my lungs, like guitar strings
when struck they make the
sweetest music
the melody bleeds and so do I
nostalgia is destructive
It renders me limbless
It renders me useless
I cannot see past the fog
of things that used to be
I crave for the honeyed water
of a river I've never seen
at last, I am nothing but a devotee
because nostalgia is just longing
and longing is just praying.

42.

the day ends
the night comes
and if no one else
has found me by then
my misery will find me
once again.

43.

give me a map of the graveyard
my life has become
so I know which tombstones not to visit
and which graves aren't worth the flowers
give me a map
of the graveyard my life has become
so I can dance over corpses of vows I broke
and sing to the ghosts of people I once knew
lead me by hand
to the graveyard
my life has become
so I can find soil, rich and lush
and plant flowers of hope.

Acknowledgements

For these poems to make it out of my notes app and into the real world, I owe my gratitude to many people firstly, I'd like to thank my parents for the incredible love and support they've shown me throughout my life, I truly could not have asked for better.

secondly, I am most grateful for my siblings, Nancy didi and Abhinav, thank you guys for always having my back. You two get me like no one else does and believe me when I say I'd give up both my kidneys for you. I wouldn't be who I am if not for the love I got from you two.

Kesar didi, thank you for helping me get through the last minute nerves and special thank you for always always being by my side. One day, I hope to have your infinite wisdom (I agree, you are a god)

Suhana, you played a big hand in me getting the courage to finally get up and write this book, thank you for always being nothing but kind to me. Yashi, since the day I met you you've had unwavering trust in my capabilities. you made me believe in myself and for that there aren't enough thank you's in the world but still, thank you.

Aastha, the best hype girl of the century award definitely goes to you, you simply are amazing. Mona, you've been such an awesome friend and I am so grateful to have you.
And to you, my beautiful reader, thank you for giving me a chance.

www.ingramcontent.com/pod-product-compliance
Lightning Source LLC
Chambersburg PA
CBHW031513150726
47990CB00007B/2997